Table Talk

FOR MY BIG, WONDERFUL FAMILY,
WITH MANY THANKS FOR
ALL THE GREAT MEALTIME CONVERSATIONS
WE'VE SHARED AROUND THE DINNER TABLE
THROUGHOUT THE YEARS

365 DINNERTIME DISCUSSION STARTERS FOR FAMILIES

JENNIFER FLANDERS

Prescott Publishing
3668 Southwood Drive
Tyler, TX 75707

© 2020 by Jennifer Flanders
All rights reserved

For more fresh ideas for family fun
plus lots of free printable resources,
please visit us online at
www.flandersfamily.info.

ISBN: 978-1-938945-44-1
(print version)

TABLE OF CONTENTS

Introduction	9
New Year's Conversation Starters	13
Winter Days Conversation Starters	17
Springtime Conversation Starters	21
Easter Conversation Starters	25
Good Neighbor Conversation Starters	29
Mealtime Conversation Starters	33
Summer Fun Conversation Starters	37
Freedom Loving Conversation Starters	41
Bible Knowledge Conversation Starters	45
Family Travel Conversation Starters	49
Back-to-School Conversation Starters	53
Hardworking Conversation Starters	57
Autumn Days Conversation Starters	61
Thanksgiving Conversation Starters	65
Christmas Conversation Starters	69
Conclusion	73

INTRODUCTION

What are mealtimes like at your house? Do you grab food on the run? Eat your meals in front of the television? Sit at the table devouring dinner in silence, with every family member absorbed in their own thoughts or glued to their digital devices?

Or maybe you have a spouse or child who tends to monopolize the conversation. Can anybody else get a word in edgewise? Perhaps the same few topics dominate every discussion: politics, pandemics, pop culture. And you're ready for a change.

If you're longing for a way to draw your family together and make your mealtimes more interactive, I can think of no better way than asking open-ended questions and giving everyone the opportunity to reply.

As a homeschool mom, I'm with most of my children all day every day. So the classic opener "tell me about your day" doesn't usually work for us. But the conversation starters listed in the following chapters have really done the trick. We use them whether we are at home by ourselves or dining with friends and extended family.

I keep a stack of the printable versions of these cards in a mason jar in the kitchen, and reach for it every night as we sit down to eat. We normally have everyone answer the same question, then move on to the next card the following night. But you could also have each person draw a different question, if you prefer to do it that way. Or read them straight out of the book, using a marker to track your progress through the different categories.

Although I created these *Table Talk* questions to foster dinner-time discussions and to encourage families to linger around the table a little longer, this resource can be used in any setting. Draw from these discussion starters before bedtime or after breakfast or while you're driving down the road. As you do, you'll be obeying one of God's most foundational and vital commands.

God charges parents to teach Biblical values to their children, "speaking of them when you sit in your house, when you walk in the way, when you lie down, and when you rise up." (see Deuteronomy 11:19) We need to be intentional about cultivating our children's faith in God. But that doesn't necessitate our lining our kids up for a lengthy lecture several times a day.

Rather, our beliefs, convictions, and values should inform everything we are and do and say. They need to be communicated in an authentic, organic way. These discussion starters provide a quick and easy way to do exactly that.

Kids are perceptive. They will soon pick up on what's most important to you, not from being told your priorities, but by observing with their own eyes how you put those priorities into action, seeing how your values dictate your decisions, and hearing how your beliefs influence not only what you say, but how you say it. This is true of conversations both casual and formal, in public and private, with friend or foe, at work or at play… or gathered around the family table.

NEW YEAR'S CONVERSATION STARTERS

1. What resolutions are you making for the coming year (if any)?

2. Which of the resolutions you made last year did you keep? Any tips for success?

3. What are you most looking forward to in the coming year?

4. What in the coming year are you most nervous about?

5. Name one new habit you'd like to develop. Who will hold you accountable?

6. What academic goals have you set for yourself in the coming year?

7. What spiritual goals have you set for yourself in the coming year?

8. Have you set any physical goals for yourself in the coming year?

9. Name a book you haven't read but plan to read this year?

10. Name a place you haven't been but would like to go this year.

11. Name a project you'd like to finish in the next twelve months.

12. Name a new skill you'd like to learn in the coming year.

13. What can you do to better serve your family this year?

14. What can you do to more faithfully share the gospel this year?

15. What will you do to better budget your time this year?

16. How are you doing on your New Year's resolutions so far?

17. What new habits do you think we should adopt to grow closer as a family this year?

18. If you had to choose one focus word for the coming year, what would it be?

19. Would you rather go to bed early on Dec. 31 or stay up to ring in the new year?

20. What activities might you cut this year to free up time for working on other goals?

21. What are your top three priorities? Why?

22. Can others tell what's most important to you by what you spend the most time doing?

23. Where would you like to see yourself in five years?

24. What can you do to help others achieve their goals?

WINTER DAYS CONVERSATION STARTERS

1. What do you like the most about cold weather?

2. What do you like the least about cold weather?

3. Share a favorite memory involving snow.

4. What's your favorite cold weather drink?

5. Do you prefer salty or sweet popcorn?

6. MLK advocated peaceful protests. Have you ever protested peacefully? Explain.

7. Name your favorite winter Olympic sport.

8. How many blankets do you keep on your bed to stay warm?

9. What's your favorite kind of hot soup?

10. Which would you prefer: hiking in the dead of winter or sitting home by a blazing fire?

11. Would you rather wear mittens or gloves? Why?

12. Share a favorite memory from Valentine's Day.

13. How many US presidents can you name?

14. What's your favorite flavor of ice cream?

15. Have you ever been the recipient of a random act of kindness? Share details.

16. Tell about a time you told the truth, even though you knew it might get you in trouble.

17. What's your favorite fairy tale? Give a brief summary.

18. If you could have any animal in the world as a pet, which would you choose?

19. Do you prefer pullover sweaters or cardigans? Describe your favorite.

20. What's your favorite kind of cake? When did you last have it?

21. What's the nicest compliment you've ever received?

22. Would you rather build a snowman or build forts for a snowball fight?

23. Dr. Seuss's birthday is March 3. Can you quote a few lines from any of his books?

24. What is your favorite kind of breakfast cereal? What do you like about it?

SPRINGTIME CONVERSATION STARTERS

1. What are your favorite springtime flowers?

2. Which spring cleaning chore most desperately needs to be done at your house?

3. What's your favorite vegetable? And your least favorite?

4. Describe a favorite park or playground you've visited.

5. Share a funny joke you've heard.

6. What's your favorite way to relieve stress?

7. If you could grow anything in a backyard garden, what would you choose?

8. If you were to die, what epitaph would you want written on your grave marker?

9. What's your least favorite household chore? Why?

10. What do you like about having siblings (if any) or about being an only child (if not).

11. If you could play any instrument you like, what would you choose?

12. What's something you can do to take better care of the earth?

13. Who's your favorite superhero? Why?

14. If you could possess any superpower, what would you choose?

15. Share something interesting about the last book you read (or one you're reading now).

16. Quote a Mother Goose rhyme from memory.

17. What's your favorite Star Wars character. Why?

18. Mother's Day is in May. What's your earliest memory of your mother?

19. Make up an original, impromptu limerick (use rhyme pattern: AABBA).

20. Have you ever gotten blamed for something you didn't do? Explain.

21. Name something popular to do in your hometown that you've never done before.

22. What's your favorite undersea animal?

23. Have you ever been fishing? Share your best fishing memory.

24. Describe a trick you've played (or want to play) on April Fool's Day.

EASTER CONVERSATION STARTERS

1. What's your favorite Easter tradition?

2. Have you ever been to a sunrise service? Would you like to attend one?

3. How would you explain the gospel to someone who's never heard it before?

4. Jesus was silent before his accusers. How do you respond when you're falsely accused?

5. How many of Jesus's twelve disciples can you name?

6. Have you ever dyed Easter eggs? What would you do with the eggs once you finished?

7. Have you given your heart to Jesus? Share your testimony.

8. Tell about a person who is especially good at making you feel loved.

9. Jesus healed 10 lepers, but only 1 thanked him. Have you ever forgotten to say thanks?

10. Joy is a fruit of the Spirit. Who is the most joyous person you know?

11. Peace is a fruit of the Spirit. Share about a time when you felt especially at peace.

12. Patience is a fruit of the Spirit. Tell about a person who's been especially patient with you.

13. Tell about a time when the person on your right showed great kindness.

14. Goodness is a fruit of the Spirit. What evidence of goodness do others see in your life?

15. Share an instance when a friend or family member remained faithful during hard times.

16. Tell about a time you've observed the person on your left act with great gentleness.

17. Tell about a friend or family member who exhibits a lot of self-control.

18. If, when you die, God asks you why He should let you into heaven, what will you say?

19. Have you ever hunted Easter eggs? Tell about the trickiest place you found one hidden.

20. Do you wear new clothes to church on Easter? Share a favorite memory about that.

21. Have you ever been baptized? Why do you suppose Jesus was baptized?

22. Explain what you know about the Lord's Supper.

23. The disciples fell asleep while Jesus prayed. Is it ever hard for you to stay awake to pray?

24. After His resurrection, Jesus issued the great commission. When's the last time you shared the gospel?

GOOD NEIGHBOR CONVERSATION STARTERS

1. What's your earliest memory of a neighbor? Tell us about it.

2. Share something that makes you grateful for the neighbors you have.

3. Who is your most like-minded, "kindred spirit" friend?

4. Name somebody in your extended family you'd like to spend more time with.

5. Brainstorm ideas for getting to know your fellow church members better.

6. Put yourself in the shoes of your grouchiest neighbor. What makes him or her so grumpy?

7. Have you ever befriended someone with whom you have little in common? Explain.

8. Brainstorm ideas for how you can better serve the people who live around you.

9. If we had to move to another town, which neighbors would you miss most. Why?

10. What's the best reason you can think of not to gossip?

11. Have you ever had a problem with a neighbor? How did you resolve it?

12. Brainstorm new ways to share the gospel with neighbors who don't know Christ.

13. Share a positive trait about each of the neighbors that surround you.

14. How can you live at peace with a neighbor who doesn't share your same values?

15. Which of your neighbors should get a "yard of the month award" for beautiful landscaping?

16. Have you ever had to have a hard conversation with a neighbor? How did it go?

17. What are the benefits/drawbacks of belonging to a homeowner's association?

18. Share a funny story involving a neighbor's pet.

19. Describe a situation with a neighbor that went badly, but that you can laugh about now.

20. If you needed to borrow a cup of sugar, which neighbor would you ask?

21. What's the most embarrassing thing your neighbor has ever caught you doing?

22. Some people say good fences make good neighbors. Would you agree or disagree?

23. The Bible tells us to love our neighbors as ourselves. Which of your neighbors is hardest to love?

24. What positive changes can you make to be a better neighbor?

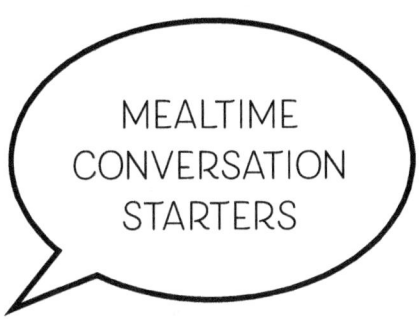

MEALTIME CONVERSATION STARTERS

1. Would you rather wash dishes or dry?

2. Did you have a "best friend" growing up? Describe that person.

3. What's your favorite Disney character? Why?

4. Do you prefer coffee or tea? How do you take it?

5. What's your favorite kind of cookies? Have you ever made them yourself?

6. Say something nice about the person on your right.

7. If you could only eat one kind of dessert for the rest of your life, what would you pick?

8. If NASA were recruiting pioneers for a new settlement on Mars, would you apply?

9. What's your favorite kind of donut?

10. How many different ways can you think of to reuse/repurpose/recycle a milk jug?

11. Which Summer Olympic sport would you be most interested in watching?

12. If you needed to wear corrective lenses, would you prefer glasses or contacts?

13. What are your favorite colors to wear and/or to look at?

14. Have you ever experienced a miracle or been helped by a "guardian angel?" Explain.

15. What's your preferred topping for an ice cream sundae?

16. Would you rather read fiction or nonfiction books?

17. Who's your favorite music artist (or classical composer)?

18. What's your favorite fast food restaurant?

19. If you had to give up one of your five senses, which would you choose?

20. Share a story you enjoy hearing your parents tell about you.

21. Do you like to cook? What's your specialty?

22. Where and what was the fanciest meal you've ever eaten?

23. Name a food you didn't like at first but eventually developed a taste for.

24. Do you follow the 5-second rule? Would you eat something you dropped on the floor?

1. What's thing are you most looking forward to doing this summer?

2. Describe a trick you played on somebody that got a better reaction than expected.

3. Would you rather swim in a pool or at the beach?

4. Name your favorite berry. Do you prefer them plain or used in a recipe?

5. Share a memory of a picnic you've taken (or plan one together now).

6. If you were to observe a "screen-free week," how would you spend it?

7. Say something nice about someone in the room.

8. Share a special memory about your dad.

9. What was your favorite childhood toy or game?

10. If you had a limitless supply of glow sticks, what would you do with them?

11. How many different ways can you think of to reuse/repurpose/recycle a glass jar?

12. Triathlons include a swim, bike, and run. Which leg of the race would be easiest for you?

13. Do you think we'll ever discover life on other planets?

14. What's your favorite sort of insect and why?

15. What artistic technique would you most like to learn?

16. If you were to donate a box of used items to charity, what's the first thing you'd put into it?

17. Name your favorite kind of "junk" food.

18. How'd you prefer to spend time outdoors: resting in a hammock or digging in a garden?

19. Do you like going to thrift shops & garage sales? What sort of stuff do you look for?

20. If you were going to tackle a self-improvement project, what would it be?

21. What are your favorite pizza toppings?

22. Have you ever been accused of lying when you were telling the truth? Explain.

23. What's the best news you've heard in the past week?

24. Do you consider yourself a "glass half-full" or "half-empty" kind of person?

1. Can you name, in order, what God made on each day of creation?

2. Name the first three sons of Adam and Eve.

3. Who was Noah and what did he do? Share everything you remember about his story.

4. What happened at the Tower of Babel?

5. How many sons did Jacob have? Who was his favorite?

6. What happened after Joseph's jealous brothers sold him into slavery?

7. Who was Moses and what did he do? Share everything you remember about his story.

Table Talk: 365 Dinnertime Discussion Starters

8. How many of the 10 commandments can you quote?

9. How did Esther become queen? What important thing did she do for her people?

10. Who killed Goliath? How and why did he do it?

11. Why did Balaam beat his donkey? How did the donkey respond?

12. Who was Jonah and what did he do? Share everything you remember about his story.

13. What happened when Elijah met the prophets of Baal on Mount Carmel?

14. Why were Shadrach, Meshach & Abednego thrown into the furnace? What happened?

15. Why was Daniel thrown into the lion's den? What happened to him there?

16. Why did an angel visit Mary? How did she respond?

17. Why did Mary & Joseph have to travel to Bethlehem? How did they end up in a stable?

18. How did the shepherds and the wise men know where to find Jesus?

19. What did Jesus use to feed five thousand? How much was left over afterwards?

20. How did John the Baptist meet his demise?

21. Explain what happened after Lazarus died. How did the pharisees react to this news?

22. Why was Jesus crucified? What happened afterwards?

23. Who wrote most of the books in the New Testament?

24. James wrote that "faith without works is dead." What does that mean?

1. Share what you know about the American Revolution.

2. If you could have dinner with three figures from American history, which ones would you choose?

3. Do you know any veterans? How can you thank them for their service to our country?

4. What do you like most about living in the USA (or whatever country you live in)?

5. Would you rather watch a fireworks display or set off sparklers and smoke bombs yourself?

6. Can you quote the Preamble to the US Constitution? If not, look it up & memorize it.

7. Do you know our national anthem? Sing the first verse.

8. If you could travel back in time to watch past US events unfold, where would you go?

9. Explain what you know about the three branches of US government.

10. If you were going to run for US president, what campaign promises would you make?

11. Do you believe it's important to vote? Why or why not?

12. Do you think some issues are too important to compromise, even for the sake of getting along?

13. Do you know the Pledge of Allegiance? Recite it now.

14. Should there be any limits on freedom of speech. If so, what should they be?

15. Some claim, "Silence is violence." In what way is that true? In what way is it false?

16. Is there a Biblical basis for "United we stand, divided we fall?" What is it?

17. Share what you know about George Washington.

18. Share what you know about Abraham Lincoln.

19. In what ways have you seen God bless America?

20. In what ways has America turned her back on God?

21. What's the difference between Communism and Free Market economics?

22. Discuss what you know about World War I.

23. Discuss what you know about World War II.

24. If you could celebrate Independence Day anywhere in America, where would you pick?

FAMILY TRAVEL CONVERSATION STARTERS

1. If you had to move to another country, which would you choose?

2. Share a favorite family vacation memory.

3. What's something you wish you'd had on your last road trip but forgot to take?

4. Which is your favorite way to travel: car, boat, plane, or train? Why?

5. Would you rather go to the mountains or the beach?

6. If you could only vacation in one spot for the rest of your life, where would it be?

7. Share a funny story from one of your family trips.

8. Would you prefer a single long vacation trip a year or lots of little trips?

9. Describe one of the most beautiful sights you've ever seen on vacation.

10. Do you favor packing lightly or being well prepared? Is there a way to do both?

11. Where would you love to go that you haven't been yet?

12. Would you prefer tent camping or staying in a cabin?

13. What's your favorite thing about long road trips?

14. What's your favorite thing about flying on airplanes?

15. Would you rather go to a National Park or an amusement park?

16. Do you collect a certain kind of souvenir? If so, what?

17. Would you rather visit a science and technology museum or an art museum?

Table Talk: 365 Dinnertime Discussion Starters

18. Have you ever gotten lost far from home? What did you have to do to find your way?

19. Would you prefer to snow ski or water ski?

20. Have you ever taken a stay-cation? What's your favorite thing to do close to home?

21. In your opinion, what is the optimal length of a vacation trip?

22. What's the most fun FREE thing you ever remember doing on vacation?

23. If you were stranded alone on a desert island, what's the first thing you'd do?

24. What's the farthest point away from home you've ever been?

BACK-TO-SCHOOL CONVERSATION STARTERS

1. Have you ever failed a test? Explain.

2. Did your school have PE? Describe the games you played during recess.

3. Describe a lab experiment or science fair project you remember doing.

4. Share a story about school pictures. Do you have any old ones?

5. Who was your favorite teacher in school? What did you like most about him/her?

6. Have you ever had a school-related nightmare? Describe one.

7. Describe a school field trip you remember.

8. Homeschooling is illegal in some countries. Why do you think that is?

9. If money were no object, would you put your kids in public, private, or homeschool?

10. If your school held a talent show, what talent would your performance highlight?

11. Did you learn to play an instrument in school? Which one? Do you still play?

12. What sports did you play (or wish you played) in school?

13. Do you complete assignments right away or procrastinate until the last minute?

14. Were you ever sent to the principal's office? Why?

15. What subject did you have the hardest time wrapping your mind around?

16. What school subject(s) come easiest to you?

17. What's the highest compliment a teacher ever paid you?

18. Did you ever do something you later regretted just because peers pressured you into it?

19. Tell about a time you did the right thing even though it was hard.

20. Did/do you love school or live for summer vacation? Why?

21. What was the most embarrassing thing that ever happened to you at school?

22. What school supplies are you happiest about replacing every August?

23. Describe school lunches. Did you bring food from home or buy lunch in the cafeteria?

24. If you could take any subject you want as an elective, what would you pick?

HARDWORKING CONVERSATION STARTERS

1. Do you consider yourself more of a minimalist or a packrat?

2. What home improvement project would you like to see done ASAP?

3. What's the most boring chore you do? How could you make it more interesting?

4. Are you a night owl or a morning person?

5. When it comes to household repairs, do you prefer to call a professional or DIY?

6. Did you make your bed this morning? Why or why not?

7. Describe the best and/or worst customer service you ever received.

8. Describe the best and/or worst customer service you ever received.

9. If you could be mentored by anybody on earth, whom would you pick?

10. If you could take lessons to learn a new skill, what would it be?

11. What chore have you been procrastinating that you should get started on TODAY?

12. Have you ever lost a job or been fired? Explain.

13. Describe a time when you had to do a job you weren't sure you could handle, but did.

14. Share a time when a boss (or parent or teacher) offered constructive criticism. How did you respond?

15. What kind of assignment at work or school makes you most nervous? Why?

16. Would you rather get detailed instructions for an assigned task or general guidelines?

17. You find out your boss is doing something shady. Do you confront him, ignore it, or quit?

18. One thing I like most about my job (or assigned chore) is…

19. Would you rather lead or follow?

20. Describe a conflict you've had with a coworker and how you handled it.

21. How should a boss deal with lazy workers? Supervise, incentivize, or fire them?

22. There are 3 keys to success: Show up. Work hard. Be nice. Which are you strongest at?

23. What motivates you to do your best work?

24. Which is more effective? Rewarding a job well done? Or punishing a sloppy worker?

AUTUMN DAYS CONVERSATION STARTERS

1. What's your favorite thing about fall?

2. Would you describe yourself as more of a cat person or a dog person?

3. Share a favorite memory involving a grandparent.

4. If you had to wear a hat, what kind of hat would you choose?

5. September 19 is "International Talk like a Pirate Day." Give it a try!

6. When's the last time you laughed so hard you cried? What was so funny?

7. How many different ways can you think of to reuse/repurpose/recycle a tin can?

Table Talk: 365 Dinnertime Discussion Starters

8. October is "Pastor Appreciation Month." What do you appreciate most about yours?

9. Coyotes howl at the moon. Give your best coyote impression.

10. Suppose you found mold on a big slab of cheese. Would you pare it off and eat the rest or toss it out?

11. How do you prefer to eat your eggs? Fried, boiled, or scrambled? Hard cooked or runny?

12. Describe an instance when your first impression proved to be wrong.

13. If you could invent anything to improve life on earth, what would it be?

14. Name your favorite kind of pasta. What sort of sauce do you like to put on it (if any)?

15. October 31 is Reformation Day. What modern-day institution most needs reform?

16. Do you prefer taking baths or showers?

17. If you were going to write a book, what would it be about?

18. Describe the nastiest thing you've ever found in the back of your fridge.

19. What's your favorite part of a slice of bread: the brown crust or the soft middle?

20. Sing the catchiest jingle you remember from a television commercial.

21. Do you prefer dill pickles or sweet?

22. If you had to eat a sandwich, what kind would you choose?

23. Tell about a special snail mail letter you've received in the past. Did you keep it?

24. Think of the biggest "cloud" in your life right now. What's the silver lining?

1. Name something you are grateful for today.

2. Share something your parents did that makes you thankful.

3. Tell about a friend for whom you are grateful and why.

4. Name something you love about the way God made you.

5. Name something you admire about the person on your left.

6. Tell what you know about America's first Thanksgiving.

7. What is something you like about living where you live?

8. Share a favorite Bible verse and tell why it's special to you.

9. Tell about a neighbor who has been a blessing to you and why.

10. Name something positive that resulted from a difficult trial. Explain.

11. What is your favorite school subject and why?

12. Name three things from childhood you are grateful for.

13. Name something you admire about the person on your right.

14. Share a lesson God is teaching you that you're glad to know.

15. Name a food you are thankful for. When did you first eat it?

16. What is your favorite pastime and why?

17. Tell about a time a stranger came to your aid in some way.

18. What is your favorite song or hymn? Sing the first verse.

Table Talk: 365 Dinnertime Discussion Starters

19. Share a funny story that always makes you laugh.

20. Tell a story about your favorite teacher.

21. Name something you love about the country you live in.

22. Tell about a time when God calmed your fears.

23. Tell about a good book you've read. What did you like about it?

24. What is your favorite movie and why?

1. Share a favorite Christmas memory.

2. What's your favorite Christmas carol? Sing the first verse of it.

3. Tell about the most memorable Christmas gift you've received.

4. What do you consider the most stressful part of the holiday season? Why?

5. If you could go anywhere in the world for Christmas, where would you go?

6. Retell a favorite Christmas story in your own words.

7. What's your earliest Christmas memory from childhood?

8. What past Christmas traditions do you wish we'd revive?

9. What can/do you do to make Christmas better for someone in need?

10. Have you ever felt fearful about receiving news that ended up being good? Explain.

11. The wise men brought gifts to Jesus. What kind of gift can you offer Him?

12. What's your favorite holiday food?

13. Have you ever been left home alone as a kid? What did you do?

14. Have you had a dream that felt like a warning from God? How did it affect your actions?

15. Would you rather attend a Christmas party or go to a Christmas parade? Why?

16. What's your favorite thing to find in your Christmas stocking?

17. What can you do personally to help bring peace on Earth?

18. Tell about a homemade gift you've given or received.

19. What's your favorite Christmas movie? Have you watched it yet this year?

20. What have you done today that would earn you a place on Santa's "nice" list?

21. Have you ever had a White Christmas? Share the most memorable.

22. Tell about a time you had to travel when you didn't feel well.

23. What might you do to bring joy to the world (or at least to your neighbors) this year?

24. What's your favorite kind of gift to give? To receive?

CONCLUSION

That about wraps up our *Dinnertime Discussion Starters for Families*. About, but not quite. I promised you a full year's worth of questions. If you read through this book cover to cover, you'll note there have been 24 questions in each of 15 topics. But since 15 x 24 = 360, that means I still owe you five more, which you'll find below.

I hope these conversation starters have been a blessing to your family. I pray they've helped foster the same kind of lively table talk at your house as they have at ours. If so, they've undoubtedly helped you get to know one another a bit better than when you began.

Now it's time to see how well you've listened. Use these last five questions to review what you've learned from the past twelve months of *Table Talk*.

1. What's the funniest story you remember from your dinnertime discussions?

2. What was the most surprising thing you learned this year?

3. Recall a favorite for everyone at the table (favorite color, dessert, movie, book, etc.).

4. Which category of questions did you enjoy most?

5. Let everyone share what they most appreciate about one person at the table. Repeat nightly until each member in your family has had a turn in the spotlight.

CHECK OUT OUR OTHER BOOKS

Get Up & Go:
Fun Ideas for Getting Fit as a Family

Sit Down & Eat:
Fun Ideas for Making Mealtimes Memorable

Pack Up & Leave:
Travel Tips for Fun Family Vacations

Balance:
The Art of Minding What Matters Most

25 Ways to Communicate Respect to Your Husband:
A Handbook for Wives

25 Ways to Show Love to Your Wife:
A Handbook for Husbands

Love Your Husband/Love Yourself:
Embracing God's Purpose for Passion in Marriage

Glad Tidings:
The First 25 Years of Flanders Family Christmas Letters

The Prodigy Project: A Novel

Moment by Moment:
A Devotional Journal for Girls

www.ingramcontent.com/pod-product-compliance
Lightning Source LLC
Chambersburg PA
CBHW060422050426
42449CB00009B/2088